# About **Catholic Social Teaching**

Les Miller

**NOVALIS**

© 2012 Novalis Publishing Inc.

Cover design: Mardigrafe
Cover illustration: Anna Payne-Krzyzanowski
Interior images: p. 7: Skjold; pp. 9, 10, 16, 39: Plaisted; pp. 19, 26: Novalis; p. 28: Ingram; p. 30: Jupiter Images; pp. 35, 44: W.P. Wittman
Layout: Mardigrafe and Audrey Wells

Published by Novalis

Publishing Office
10 Lower Spadina Avenue, Suite 400
Toronto, Ontario, Canada
M5V 2Z2

Head Office
4475 Frontenac Street
Montréal, Québec, Canada
H2H 2S2
www.novalis.ca

Cataloguing in Publication is available from Library and Archives Canada.

We acknowledge the financial support of the Government of Canada through the Canada Book Fund for business development activities.

5  4  3  2  1        16  15  14  13  12

# TABLE OF CONTENTS

# A Word from the Author

Much of this book was written during a trip I took to India to work with children who had very little. I walked through the streets of Kolkata (Calcutta), prayed at Blessed Mother Teresa's tomb, played with homeless children, and saw where migrant child labourers go to school on a tarpaulin under a tree.

In this book you will read about how Jesus calls us to act in a loving and compassionate way. Through social justice, we can help people live in a way that is just, where their needs are met and they are treated with dignity and respect. Those seeking social justice look at the lives of people who face injustice. Social justice asks questions: What is going on? Why is it going on? What can we do to help? How can we change things to reduce injustice?

The Loreto Sisters and their lay helpers run schools in India. They are shining examples of how Catholics can help to reduce the suffering of people around the world. I would like to thank the Sisters and their helpers for showing me the face of poverty, but also the faces of joy and hope. Despite their suffering, the children were very warm and welcoming. As you read this book, don't forget Katchen, who doesn't want to live in a 3-metre-square home made of cardboard and plastic sheets. Think of Saji, who wants to learn her numbers and alphabet instead of making bricks in 40-degree heat.

Many groups of young people also bring messages of joy and hope to others. "Luke 4:18" at the York Catholic District School Board is dedicated to raising awareness about injustice in Canada and around the world. (To find out why they chose this name for themselves, see Question 5 in this book.) It has been my privilege to walk with them for 12 years. This book is dedicated to them and other Catholic social groups.

Les Miller

# What is social justice?

**A**round the world and in our own communities, we find people who have been hurt because of war and violence, poverty and neglect, discrimination and hatred, as well as pollution and climate change. When violence, greed, hatred and fear rule people's lives, our society is wounded. These kinds of injustice – where groups of people are not treated fairly or with dignity – go against what Jesus taught. Social justice is a set of attitudes and actions that tries to heal these problems. (Personal injustice is something different: it affects individuals rather than groups. If one person hits another, that is a personal wrong. But if the actions of one group cause harm to another group – for example, if polluting by one group makes things worse for others – that is social injustice.)

Injustices have been part of human history for thousands of years. In ancient books, including the Bible, we read about wars, slaves, people being sent away from their own home-land, environmental problems, famines and poverty. The Bible (and later the Church) insisted that God's people must look after victims of injustice. In 1840, Fr. Luigi Taparelli first used the term "social justice." Although this term was developed in the Roman Catholic Church, countless others have used it to describe their work to overcome such problems.

POVERTY AND HOMELESSNESS ARE ROOTED IN SOCIAL INJUSTICE.

The Church brings about social justice in different ways. It raises awareness of the issue by teaching people about injustice. One way to help is to give money to groups that help people who are suffering. This is sometimes called **charity**. We may also take action to ask why the injustice is happening. For example, we can write letters to our political leaders to tell them about our concerns and request their help. Governments and other organizations can create laws and regulations to improve the situation.

## What Old Testament figures modelled social justice?

Throughout the Bible, we find people who acted for social justice. They are role models for us today and challenge us to stand up for justice.

The family of Jacob, the Israelites, had settled in Egypt at the invitation of the Pharaoh. Four hundred years later, they had grown in number. Many became slaves. Pharaoh was afraid of their power, as there were so many of them. He ordered two Egyptian women, called Shiprah and Puah, to kill all firstborn male children as soon as they were born. The women refused, and instead helped to send the children to safety. These women teach us that we must never help those who harm others.

Moses was an Israelite baby boy who escaped death. His mother placed him in a basket made of reeds and set it on the water, and he was rescued by the princess and raised as an Egyptian prince. After killing a cruel slave master, Moses escaped into the wilderness. Here he was called by God to return to Egypt to lead the Israelite slaves to freedom and guide them to the land God had promised to them. They found freedom with God's miraculous help. Moses' story teaches us about the importance of freedom. Today there are still many types of slavery. Some people, including children, are forced to work for little or no wages. Others are like slaves because they don't have the basic rights that people need to be happy. These rights include having food, clean water, shelter and education.

After the Israelites settled in the Promised Land, prophets appeared. The people and their leaders sometimes refused to take care of people in need, such as the sick, orphans and widows. Prophets bravely challenged the powerful to remember God's command to be people of justice. Some prophets were driven out of the town or even killed for standing up to the people in power. We are also called to be prophets who remind each other to take care of one another, particularly those who are treated badly.

 The prophet Micah tells us, "What does the Lord require of you but to do justice, and to love kindness, and to walk humbly with your God?" (Micah 6:8). These are words for Christians to live by.

JONAH TRIED TO ESCAPE HIS CALLING AS A PROPHET. HE ENDED UP BEING SWALLOWED BY A BIG FISH, WHICH THEN BROUGHT HIM TO THE CITY WHERE HE WAS TO TELL THE PEOPLE TO TURN BACK TO GOD.

# 3

# How is Mary a model of justice?

An angel told Mary that she was to give birth to Jesus. It would have been difficult for her to sort out her feelings. On one hand she was blessed to have God's son growing within her. On the other hand she was a young woman, pregnant and not yet married to Joseph. Yet she says yes to God's plan and finds great joy in her pregnancy. When she visits her cousin Elizabeth, Mary sings a beautiful hymn to God called the Magnificat. Her song is full of thanksgiving to God for giving her a son who will bring justice and give power to the downtrodden.

This hope helped carry her through a difficult time when Jesus was born. Mary and Joseph were homeless, and Jesus' life was in danger because of King Herod's plan to kill all male children under the age of two. (He had heard that a new king, Jesus, had been born, and didn't want the child to grow up and replace him as king.) The Holy

MARY'S MAGNIFICAT BEGINS WITH THESE WORDS:
"MY SOUL PROCLAIMS THE GLORY OF THE LORD!" (LUKE 1:47)

Family had to flee the country and become refugees in Egypt. They knew all too well what life was like for people who were persecuted.

John's Gospel tells us about the beginning of Jesus' work with the people of Galilee. Mary and Jesus were attending a wedding in the village of Cana. When the wine ran out, Mary asked her son to solve the problem and to serve others. Mary also asks us to serve others. People of justice serve one another.

Mary served Jesus and the apostles later in the Gospels. At the foot of the cross, Mary held her crucified son in her arms.

Michelangelo's famous statue named *La Pietà* shows Mary cradling her beloved son after he has died. The sculpture, which was created over 500 years ago, is in St. Peter's Basilica in Rome. You can find photographs of it on the Internet.

# 4

## What does the Lord's Prayer teach us about justice?

Think about the words of the Lord's Prayer. Among other things, it is a prayer for justice. Look at the first word:

*Our.* Not *My* Father, but *Our* Father. We are all children of the same Father in Heaven.

We pray, *your kingdom come.* We are praying for a world where God's will for justice, peace and harmony rules, a world where greed, fear and hatred no longer exist. God's kingdom is already happening now, and we can help make it happen.

We pray for *our daily bread.* We are each praying to get our fair share of resources. Again the word *our* is used. We are asking that there be enough for all. Those who have more than they need are asked to share with those who do not have enough.

We pray for peace when we say *forgive us our trespasses as we forgive those who trespass against us.* ("Trespasses" is another word for "sins," actions that hurt our relationship with God, with others and with ourselves.) Jesus taught us that forgiveness is a path to peace between people. Forgiveness comes from understanding the other, rather than blaming the other. When you have hurt someone, tell them you are sorry for hurting them, then ask for their forgiveness.

We pray to God to save us from times of trial (*lead us not into temptation*). Finally, we pray, *deliver us from evil.* Evil shows its ugly face in injustice and countless other ways. We ask God to lead us into the light of God's love, away from evil.

 The *Catechism of the Catholic Church* teaches that "The Lord's Prayer is truly the summary of the whole gospel." (#2774)

# Why are some social justice groups called "Luke 4:18"?

Some schools have started social justice groups called Luke 4:18. Members work for justice in different ways. (We will look at a few projects in Question 24.) Their name comes from a key Gospel passage that helps us to see that Jesus asks all of us to work for justice.

In Luke 4:18, Jesus stands in a synagogue in his hometown of Nazareth. He is reading a passage from the prophet Isaiah to those who are gathered with him. Jesus reads,

> "The Spirit of the Lord is upon me, because he has anointed me to bring good news to the poor. He has sent me to proclaim release to the captives and recovery of sight to the blind, to let the oppressed go free ...."

Jesus is telling us that he is on the side of justice. His path is to serve the poor, the captives, the blind and the oppressed. If we say that we are Christians, followers of Christ, then that is our path, too. Students and teachers who follow this path as members of Luke 4:18 groups continue the justice work of Jesus.

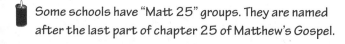

Some schools have "Matt 25" groups. They are named after the last part of chapter 25 of Matthew's Gospel.

# What messages of justice can we find in the Parable of the Good Samaritan?

Jesus told a story of a Jewish traveller who was robbed and beaten and left on the side of the road to die. As he lay bleeding, first one and then another religious leader passed him by. Although their minds were full of holy words, they didn't stop to help the victim. A third traveller, a Samaritan, did stop. People from Samaria did not get along with Jewish people. It was surprising that a Samaritan would stop and help a Jew, take care of his wounds and find him a place to stay for the night.

This parable tells us that it takes more than religious learning and devout worship to be a good person. We must make our faith and learning speak through our actions. The Samaritan may not have had as much education as the Pharisee or the devout worship of the Levite, but he knew that nothing is more important than helping our neighbour in need.

The Samaritan is a stranger to the victim and the passers-by, yet he helps. This story challenges us to look at people we think of as different or even as enemies. We must look beyond their reputation or stereotype and take action.

Another story about justice, found in Luke's Gospel, is the Parable of Lazarus and the Rich Man (Luke 16:19-31). Look it up and think about its message.

## CATHOLICS AND SOCIAL JUSTICE

# What Catholic saints and heroes modelled social justice?

Every saint teaches us about justice. All saintly people show us how to live justly by seeking good relationships with God and with other people. Many set an example for us through noble acts of helping victims of violence and poverty. Let's take a brief look at how the work of some of these saints and heroes continues today.

St. Francis of Assisi (1181–1226) cared for the poor and the sick. (Read more about him in *25 Questions about Catholic Saints and Heroes.*) After his death, his Franciscan friends continued his work by setting up shelters for the homeless and running food banks for the needy. They are still at work in the world today. Francis is also a patron saint of the environment. Social justice includes care for creation.

Women such as Blessed Mary Ward (1585–1645) and St. Rose Venerini (1656–1728) saw that young women who were poor had little chance of improving their lives without an education. At that time, many girls did not go to school. Rose Venerini and Mary Ward set up schools for girls. Today, religious orders continue this work of education. They include the Venerini Sisters (founded by St. Rose) and the Loretto sisters (founded by Mary Ward).

ST. FRANCIS IS OFTEN PORTRAYED WITH BIRDS AND ANIMALS, WHICH ARE GOD'S CREATURES.

Other Catholic saints and heroes to investigate include St. Vincent de Paul, St. Gianna Beretta Molla, Dorothy Day, Thomas Merton, Blessed Mother Teresa, and Archbishop Oscar Romero. Beyond the Catholic tradition, other notable justice figures include Gandhi, Martin Luther King Jr., and Nelson Mandela.

# Why does the Catholic Church work for social justice?

The Catholic Church often challenges unjust systems or governments. The Church urges nations that are at war to find a peaceful solution to their problems. It asks governments of wealthy nations to help poorer countries. The Church also speaks up for people who are unemployed, in prison, or dealing with the effects of climate change. The Catholic Church has played an important role in countries where political freedom is limited, such as in Poland in the 1980s. Pope John Paul II was a key figure in world events at that time.

Life might be easier for Catholics if we kept quiet about justice issues. But we can't be silent when people and the earth are not treated fairly and with dignity, because then we would stop being followers of Christ's teachings. The Church continues to teach the Golden Rule ("In everything do to others as you would have them do to you" – Matthew 7:12). This rule for living values peace and justice over war and oppression (Matthew 5:3-12). It seeks to care for the sick, the homeless, the hungry and the imprisoned (Matthew 25:35-45). All of these directions came from Jesus. If the Church stopped doing these things, then all the beautiful worship and deeply felt prayers would be hypocritical. Jesus warned against saying one thing but not following up on our words with action.

Jesus also taught us about the virtue of compassion (see John 11:33-35 for an example of Jesus showing compassion). When we are deeply moved by the suffering of another person, that is called empathy. When that empathy leads us to help people who suffer, this is compassion. Compassion is at the heart of many of our justice works.

## How does the Catholic Church teach about social justice?

As we have seen, the Bible contains many teachings about justice. The Church applies these teachings to today's world. At large gatherings called Ecumenical Councils, the bishops of the Church agree on many important aspects of Church life, including justice issues. The Catholic Church teaches about social justice through encyclicals, which are letters the Pope writes to the Church. Papal encyclicals have shaped Catholic thinking on justice in our world. They explore difficult social issues such as war in the nuclear age, environmental threats, the duties of governments to citizens, the rights of workers, and the rights of employers.

Bishops, priests and Catholic groups discuss these teachings and then find ways to apply them in their local communities. In Canadian Catholic schools, many of these teachings are part of the curriculum.

The best way to teach about social justice is to *do* social justice. Rather than just talking about what's wrong in the world, we learn by serving the homeless, feeding the hungry, caring for the sick, asking why there is poverty in a wealthy world – and then acting to change things. The Catholic Church

supports its teachings on justice through Development and Peace (D&P). Organizations like D&P make a difference to people's lives in lots of ways: running HIV/AIDS clinics in Africa, opening hostels for the homeless in North America, building schools for the poor in Asia, finding peaceful solutions to gang violence in South America, and pushing governments to protect the rights of children in Europe.

FOR THIS SOUTH AMERICAN BOY, POVERTY IS A WAY OF LIFE.

# What are the works of mercy?

The spiritual and corporal works of mercy are ways of helping the poor that also bring us closer to God. Mercy means "God's healing love." Spiritual works of mercy help the minds and souls of the poor. Corporal works are actions that help the physical well-being of the poor. ("Corporal" comes from the Latin word *corpus*, which means "body.") We are called to do these works all our lives. The list below shows each work along with an explanation or an example you can try.

## The spiritual works of mercy

- Instruct the uninformed. (Teach people what they need to know to grow as God's children.)
- Counsel the doubtful. (Give advice to people who are not sure God loves them.)
- Admonish sinners. (If there are people who are doing something wrong on purpose, help them see that it is wrong.)
- Bear wrongs patiently. (When someone laughs at you or tells lies about you, be strong and keep following Jesus.)
- Forgive offenses willingly. (Forgive people who have hurt you and start fresh.)

- Comfort the afflicted. (Bring kindness and hope to those who are suffering.)
- Pray for the living, the sick and the dead. (Remember these people in your prayers.)

## The corporal works of mercy

- Feed the hungry. (Bring items to a food drive.)
- Give drink to the thirsty. (Support clean water campaigns for those in poorer parts of the world who get diseases from dirty drinking water.)
- Shelter the homeless. (Raise money for a homeless shelter in your community.)
- Clothe the naked. (Donate clothes during clothing drives.)
- Visit the imprisoned. (Personal visits are usually tasks for adults, but young people can write letters of support to people who are put in prison because of their religious beliefs.)
- Visit the sick. (Go to see a friend who is sick, bringing news from school.)
- Bury the dead. (Go to a funeral home or funeral to comfort a friend or relative who has lost a loved one.)

Which works of mercy have you done? Which new ones can you try?

# Why is the goodness of the human person a key part of Church teaching about justice?

Catholics believe that every person is created and loved by God. Every person holds God's love inside them. Every person is sacred. While we all make bad choices at times, God still loves us.

This Church teaching is based on the Bible. In the Book of Genesis, which tells the stories of God creating the world, human beings are made in God's image. God breathes his spirit into the first human. Later, Jesus teaches us that we are his brothers and sisters. We are all members of God's family.

Catholic social teaching is built on this view that we are all part of God's family. Whenever someone is being treated unjustly, it is a sin against the person and a sin against God. Because we are God's creation, whenever we treat someone badly, we hurt our relationship with God. This special relationship with God gives each person dignity. Dignity is the sense that a person is good, is loved by God and is worthy of respect. When we do things to harm human dignity, in others or in ourselves, we are doing acts of injustice.

 All Catholic social teachings are concerned with human dignity.

# What does the Church teach about the environment?

In recent years, the Pope and the bishops have taught that everybody needs to take responsibility for the environment. Problems such as climate change, pollution, dirty drinking water, and the extinction of animal and plant species have become major concerns. The Church reminds us that we need to change our actions, but we also must change our attitudes towards nature.

Both Blessed Pope John Paul II and Pope Benedict XVI have called for ecological conversion. In other words, we need to think about creation and take action to help creation heal. Conversion is powered by God's love. Both Popes believe that being open to God's will regarding creation can help save our planet.

- We need to convert from thinking that our planet is an unlimited treasure trove of resources to working as caretakers of a beautiful creation.

- We need to convert from thinking that only human beings have rights on this planet and must work to protect all life forms.

- We need to convert from thinking that we can pollute the sky, land and water and instead work to reduce gases that are warming up our planet, stop cutting down forests, and avoid dumping sewage into rivers and lakes.

The Vatican (the headquarters of the Church, in Rome) has built solar panels on the roofs of some of its buildings so it uses fewer power sources that cause pollution. It is also seeking to grow forests to help reduce gases that are warming the planet.

Pope Benedict XVI wrote, "If you want to cultivate peace, protect creation." What do you think he meant?

The Canadian bishops published pastoral letters on the environment in 2003 and 2008.

??????????? **13** ????????

# What does the Church teach about clean water?

Two of the major causes of death in poorer countries are dysentery and cholera. These diseases cause fever, stomach pains and diarrhea. Both are caused by drinking water that contains harmful bacteria and viruses. Other deaths are caused by parasites found in the water. Worms may grow inside people's intestines. These worms live on food the person eats, causing him or her to slowly starve, even though they would normally be getting enough food. Children are at special risk for these diseases.

There are two ways to treat these problems. The first is with medicine. Vaccinations can help prevent these diseases. Or, if someone is dehydrated from severe diarrhea, rehydration salts can help them recover quickly. A second approach is to make sure people have clean water to drink. In cities, this means ensuring clean water is available to all people, especially in poorer areas, where these diseases are more common. In rural areas, it might mean drilling wells to provide clean drinking water.

The Church teaches that both approaches should be used. We need to treat the sick with as much care as possible. The Catholic Church and its missionaries is one of the largest groups to provide this medical care to those around the world who are ill. The Church also stresses that disease must be prevented in the first place. This approach finds ways to bring clean water to communities that need it, but also looks at what might stop a group from getting it. For example, a city may not want to raise taxes to build a clean water treatment facility for poorer areas. The next step is to think of ways to solve these problems. For example, local churches and the bishop may persuade city government authorities that spending money on water treatment facilities is good for everyone and for the city as a whole.

Even in Canada, access to clean drinking water is a problem in some areas, such as on Aboriginal reservations or in remote places in the North. The Catholic Church has a responsibility to reach out across the country and across the world to help those who are suffering. Development and Peace supports partner groups in certain countries through funding and training to help them deal with problems in their area.

DEVELOPMENT AND PEACE WORKS WITH PARTNERS AROUND THE WORLD TO PROVIDE CLEAN WATER.

Diarrheal disease is the second-highest cause of death in children under five years old. The leading cause of death is a lung infection called pneumonia.

# What does the Church teach about global warming?

*G*lobal warming may not sound like a bad idea in the middle of a cold Canadian winter, but it is actually a serious problem. Scientists have noticed that the average temperature on earth has been slowly rising since the Industrial Revolution (1750–1850). This is causing polar ice to melt and seawater levels to rise. Higher water levels can cause flooding in many communities along the seacoast. Hotter temperatures have also led to the increase in the size of deserts and a decrease in grasslands and forests. These are often important farming areas. When this happens, not enough food is produced and people begin to starve. Africa has had several major famines over the past few years. Scientists predict that if global warming continues, even more drastic problems will arise. Because we all share the same planet, what happens in one part of the world affects the whole world. Here's one example of global warming that you may have noticed: fewer days of skating on outdoor hockey rinks.

Global warming is mostly caused by the burning of fossil fuels, and industrialized nations such as Canada and the United States are responsible for a lot of the problem. Burning these

A FACTORY SPEWS POLLUTION INTO THE AIR.

fuels (coal, oil and gas) in our cars, homes, planes and factories releases gases into the air that trap the sun's heat. The earth becomes like a greenhouse, which uses glass to hold the sun's heat inside the building to keep plants warm. That's why these gases are called greenhouse gases.

The Church teaches that to solve this problem, we must rely less on fossil fuels. We need to find ways of driving less often and using less heat in the winter and less air conditioning in the summer. The less energy we use, the less we create greenhouse gases. We can also reduce greenhouse gases by planting forests that absorb some of the gases. As Catholics, we are called to care for our planet, reducing the harm done to keep it safe for our children and grandchildren.

 The Church has said that greed is one of the spiritual sins that causes many ecological problems. The more we want something, the more energy and resources we need to provide that thing. We have to ask ourselves, "Are the things we want worth the damage to the earth?"

The Church believes that all human life, which is a gift from God, is sacred. Let's look at some key life moments to understand what the Church teaches about them.

# Why is abortion an important issue for Catholics?

Some couples who are not ready to welcome a new baby into their lives decide that the child should be aborted. They go to a hospital or medical clinic for a procedure that ends the pregnancy.

The Catholic Church sees abortion as the wrong choice, and as a deeply sinful one, because a human life is at stake. Catholics take a strong stand against abortion because they understand that life begins when the mother's ova (egg) and the father's sperm unite to create new life. This is called **conception**. This is a special moment because God has allowed new life to begin.

Abortion is wrong because it rejects God's will, which is that the child should live. The Church knows that pregnancy can make life difficult for some people, particularly for women, but it teaches that the right to life is more important than any difficulties and challenges that the parents may face.

Children growing within the womb cannot speak or protect themselves from abortion. The Church tries to speak for the unborn, as it speaks for other groups with little or no power, such as refugees, the elderly and the poor.

MANY GROUPS OFFER SUPPORT TO YOUNG MOTHERS SO THEY CAN BUILD A HAPPY AND HEALTHY LIFE FOR THEIR BABIES.

Some women become pregnant while still in their teens, before they are married. They may feel abandoned and over-whelmed by the pregnancy. Instead of having an abortion, they can bravely reach out for help. Family members, friends or Catholic organizations can support them through the pregnancy and after the baby is born.

 One of the key Bible passages that people use to defend against abortion is from Deuteronomy 30:19: "Choose life."

# What does the Church teach about assisted death?

As we saw earlier, preserving human dignity is one of the main principles of Catholic social teaching. Respecting human dignity includes the right to a natural death. That is why we do not have the right to help someone to end his or her own life. This is called assisted suicide. If family or medical staff makes the decision to end the person's life, it is called **euthanasia.** Catholic teaching tells us that we do not have the right to take someone's life in these circumstances. We can't remove life support if a person can still think and feel. When it is clear that the person is dying, and that the ability to think and feel will not return, medical staff do not need to do extraordinary things to keep the person alive. The person's physical state will show when the natural end of life has come.

In some countries, including Canada, some people want to allow assisted suicide. Some countries also allow euthanasia in certain cases. The Church teaches that humans cannot take God's role in ending lives. While it has great compassion for the suffering that many go through as death approaches, the Church is committed to giving a voice to those who are too ill to speak for themselves. The stand of the Church in protecting the rights of the dying is based on its belief in the sacredness of life.

 In his 1995 encyclical, *Evangelium vitae* (The Gospel of Life), Pope John Paul II calls people to choose life and to turn away from practices that end life before its time.

# Where do Catholics stand on capital punishment?

*C*apital punishment is the execution of criminals who have committed a serious crime, such as murder. The Church teaches that each country has the right to set criminal sentences that it thinks are correct. But Catholics also believe that a criminal doesn't lose his or her essential humanity, no matter how bad the crime. As a human being and God's creation, the prisoner should not be mistreated. In recent years, the Church has taught that only in the most extreme circumstances should the death penalty be used.

Many countries, such as Canada, have already stopped capital punishment because of concerns about the right of the state to deliberately take a person's life. People used to think that the death penalty prevented violent crimes. But statistics show that this is not true. A better way of preventing crime is to reduce access to weapons. In other countries, capital punishment is still permitted. For example, in some states in the United States it is still allowed, even though many American Catholics and their bishops have campaigned to end the death penalty.

Canada formally abolished the death penalty in 1976, but the last execution was in 1962.

Two key figures in the fight against the death penalty in the United States were Cardinal Joseph Bernadin and Sister Helen Prejean. Sister Helen's story became an award-winning movie, *Dead Man Walking*.

**18**

## How can we work for peace in our world?

It may seem impossible to bring about peace in our world, when there are so many conflicts. Let us look at one person who changed history using a peaceful approach.

Mohandas K. Gandhi (1869–1948) is seen as the father of modern India. He led a series of campaigns against British rule in India from the 1920s until India's independence in 1947. His approach was different from many others who wanted political freedom. Instead of choosing the path of violence, he used peaceful acts of defiance to convince the British that they did not have the ability and moral right to govern India. He led marches even though they were banned, called for strikes and boycotts, and led many peaceful protests. In this way, he was able to bring peaceful change to India.

Gandhi also thought we should employ peaceful means of becoming better people. One of his famous sayings is "Be the change you want to see in the world." This means that if you want peace in the world, you must be a peaceful person. We make our hearts more peaceful by deepening our relationship with Jesus. We can do this through prayer. (See *25 Questions about Prayer* for ways of deepening your prayer life.)

Being a peaceful person also means bringing peace into our relationships. Sometimes our friends or family members do things that make us angry. A peaceful person doesn't allow their anger to become violent. Instead, they stop, pause and seek to understand why they are angry. The peaceful person seeks understanding over anger. This approach does not mean letting other people take advantage of you, but asks that you deal with injustices peacefully rather than using harsh words and violent actions as weapons.

HOW CAN YOU BRING PEACE TO YOUR RELATIONSHIPS?

 One of the titles for Jesus is "Prince of Peace."

 Gandhi was a powerful influence on Martin Luther King Jr.
He used Gandhi's peaceful approach to work for equal rights
for African Americans in the United States about 50 years ago.

# What is a human right?

We have seen that each person has a special human dignity that is rooted in our relationship with God. Almost all countries recognize that humans have basic human rights. These include the right to food, clean water, education, health care and religion. The United Nations passed a Universal Declaration of Human Rights on December 10, 1948. Later the UN made special statements about the rights of children. Knowing our rights is important. When a right is taken away, it is a sign that there is injustice. Knowing where human rights are not respected helps us to know where we need to focus our work for justice.

As Christians, we believe that not only do humans have human *rights*, but we also have human *responsibilities*. We take care of our neighbours and ourselves. In a world where we are so connected to one another by technology, we are all neighbours. We see this in times of great disasters. When earthquakes cause a huge loss of life and property, or governments use force against their people, Christians help out neighbours on the other side of the planet. And we are called to care for these brothers and sisters at all times, not just when there is a crisis.

Catholics were writing about human rights for centuries before the United Nations Declaration on Human Rights was written. The Catholic vision of human rights is found in Pope John XXIII's 1963 encyclical, *Pacem in terris* (Peace on Earth).

**20**

# Where do we find poverty in the world?

Poverty is everywhere. Most of the poor in the world live in developing countries in Asia, Africa, and South and Central America. Many of them now live in large cities, because there is not enough work to support people in rural areas. They lack proper food, have health problems and don't have much education. Many of the poor do not have the opportunity to escape poverty. They may not have enough education to get a well-paying job. Many poor people drink from polluted water, which carries diseases. If you are sick, it is hard to work and go to school. Because it is difficult to escape, this is sometimes called the **poverty trap.**

We also find poverty in Canada. As we will see in Question 23, many Aboriginal people live in poverty. There are also pockets of poverty in every province. Newcomers to our country, single women with children, elderly people, and some other groups also have higher rates of poverty.

The Catholic Church has worked to help the poor for centuries. Jesus taught that he was particularly to be found among the poor. Saints such as Vincent de Paul (1581–1660) gave us examples of how we can help the poor. Church teaching says that whenever we have a choice between helping those who have enough money and those who don't, we should help the poor. This belief is put into action among the poor around the world. The Catholic Church continues to help many people through its hospitals, clinics and schools. Many of these are run by priests, sisters and brothers as well as their **lay** co-workers.

 The St. Vincent de Paul Society is still doing this good work of serving the poor. Check out their website to find out more.

# Where does the Church stand on the rights of women?

Less than a century ago, women in Canada did not have the right to vote in elections. Husbands were seen as the head of the household. Most women did not work outside the home. If a woman did work at the same job as a man, she was usually paid less money. Over time, the rights of women have improved in Canada and are closer to equality with men's rights. But there are still many places in the world and even in the Church where women's rights have not been recognized.

The Catholic Church supports equal rights for voting and earning wages. Within the Church, women are playing a greater role. Some act as advisors to the Pope and the bishops. Some women study and teach **theology**. At Mass, there can be female altar servers, readers and ministers of communion.

The Church teaches that men and women should have equal rights but also distinctive roles. Priests are male because Jesus and his apostles were male. The Blessed Virgin Mary holds a very important role within the Roman Catholic Church. We find statues and pictures of Mary in churches and Catholic homes. Mary herself is a model of faith, and as we saw in Question 3, she is a model of justice.

THIS GREEK ICON OF MARY AND THE CHILD JESUS INVITES US TO PRAY AND MEDITATE.

Women have played important roles within the Church since the very beginning. Mary Magdalene was the first to see the risen Christ; Mary, the mother of Jesus, was among the disciples at Pentecost; deaconesses baptized new Christians in the early Church; and there are many women saints, including St. Monica, St. Clare of Assisi, St. Joan of Arc, St. Teresa of Avila, St. Marguerite Bourgeoys, and St. Thérèse of Lisieux. The first North American Aboriginal saint is a woman: St. Kateri Tekakwitha.

## 22

# What is racism?

An African Canadian applies for a job. A Canadian of European descent also applies. Both are equally qualified, but the person of European descent gets the job because the interviewer has a bias against African Canadians. This is **racism** in action.

Racism is mistreating a group of people because of negative attitudes towards them. Negative attitudes go hand in hand with stereotypes, where all people of a group are labelled with the same characteristics. **Racial discrimination** is a set of actions based on race. In Nazi Germany during the Second

World War, discrimination against Jewish people appeared in many forms. Jews were forced to wear a yellow star sewn on their clothing and were not allowed to own a business. Discrimination turned into **genocide** when six million Jewish people were killed because of their race.

The Catholic Church teaches that racism is sinful. Believing that one group is superior to another would mean we don't share equal dignity. But all people are loved by God, no matter what race or ethnic group they belong to. As we saw in the story of the Good Samaritan in Question 6, we are all neighbours.

 The Roman Catholic Church recognizes saints from many cultures around the world, including St. Paul Miki from Japan, St. Josephine Bakhita from Ethiopia, St. Rose of Lima from Peru, St. Cuthbert from the United Kingdom, and St. Kateri Tekakwitha from Canada and the United States.

## 23

# How have Aboriginal people suffered social injustice?

When Europeans settled the Americas, they found an extensive and well-developed **Aboriginal** culture. The

Europeans did not understand this culture and thought that European ideas and customs were better. They not only took over the land, they also forced many Aboriginal people to move from their own land to reserves. Aboriginal people were taught that their ways of life were not good enough. Many had difficulty adjusting to the Canadian settlers' ways of living.

The Canadian government had a plan to make Aboriginal people part of mainstream culture. Many children were forced to leave their homes to go to boarding schools, called residential schools. These were run by governments and churches, including the Roman Catholic Church. Students were taught to dress and speak like Canadians of European descent. If they spoke their own language, they were punished. Many of these children were homesick and were mistreated by school staff. In recent years, governments and churches have apologized for these injustices at residential schools.

Today, the living conditions of many Aboriginal people are far below Canadian standards. But the gifts of wisdom that First Nations, Métis and Inuit people can share with Canadians are being recognized. For example, Aboriginal people are important teachers about our relationship with creation. They teach us that if we improve our relationship with creation, we can heal some of the environmental problems we are facing.

Many Aboriginal people became Roman Catholics. They often use elements from their culture in worship services. Some use a ritual called "smudging" during the opening part of the Mass, when we tell God we are sorry for what we have done wrong.

## ORGANIZING FOR JUSTICE

# What can my school or parish do to support social justice?

Your school or parish can help the world become a more just and peaceful place. There are many examples of Canadian youth raising awareness about justice issues and developing projects to help those in need. Young people have spoken out against child labour and have spread the word about giving people access to clean water. Here are some activities that young people at schools and parishes have done:

- Collecting food for the local food bank;
- Signing a pledge not to use plastic water bottles;

- Supporting orphanages and schools in Africa, Latin America and Asia;
- Preparing meals for a homeless shelter;
- Cleaning garbage from a local area;
- Singing and visiting at a senior citizens' home;
- Inviting Development and Peace and other guest speakers to come and talk about justice issues;
- Creating school supply kits for students in poor areas;
- Twinning their school with a school in need in Canada or in a developing country;
- Writing to political leaders at home and abroad to raise concerns about specific injustices; and
- Holding Christmas toy drives for families in need.

VOLUNTEERING AT A FOOD BANK IS A GOOD WAY TO HELP PROMOTE SOCIAL JUSTICE IN YOUR COMMUNITY.

Some of these activities raise awareness, some support just action, and some give direct aid to the suffering.

 If you want to start a justice group, meet with your friends and a supportive teacher or other adult. Use a method called "See, Judge, Act" to look at social justice issues. *See*: Find out information about the issue. *Judge*: Explore what is the best action to take to tackle the issue. *Act*: Carry out the plan, and then evaluate how successful it was.

# What are some Canadian Catholic groups that support social justice?

*C*anada's Catholic bishops have supported social justice in countless ways over the years. They uphold the rights of the unborn, the dying, the poor and workers by speaking to government officials and educating the public. They have also made strong statements about ecological issues, and they support the work of Catholic groups. Local bishops have also supported justice issues, such as the rights of Aboriginal peoples, unemployment, and the negative effects of developing Alberta's oil sands.

The Canadian bishops support the work of Development and Peace (D&P), which works to support groups in poorer countries as they deal with injustice. D&P also educates the Canadian public about injustice and supports organizations that are looking for social change. It works with school and parish groups to raise awareness about poverty, ecological issues and other injustices. D&P is also part of a worldwide justice group called Caritas Internationalis. When a disaster strikes, D&P sends donations to its international partners.

Many smaller organizations are also working to build a more just world. Religious orders support various needs: the **Jesuits** provide education, the Loreto Sisters in India work with the homeless, and the Franciscans help the hungry. They also have international connections. For example, the Loretto Sisters in Canada have set up projects around the world to help the poor free themselves from the poverty trap.

As Catholics, we are all asked to get involved in social justice. Every effort is needed and valuable. Think of some ways you can make a difference at school, at your parish and in your community. Get your friends, family and neighbours involved and start changing the world!

Aboriginal Canadians: First Nations, Inuit and Métis people.

*Catechism of the Catholic Church:* A summary of the official teachings of the Roman Catholic Church.

Charity: Usually it means giving money to a group to support its justice work. It also means bringing God's love to the world.

Compassion: Feeling empathy for another person's suffering and acting to relieve that suffering.

Conception: The beginning of human life.

Corporal: Refers to the body.

Dignity: The sense that we are all good people, loved by God and worthy of respect.

Ecological conversion: Changing our attitudes and actions to protect creation.

Ecumenical Council: A worldwide gathering of bishops that defines Church teachings.

Empathy: Feeling what another person may be feeling.

Euthanasia: Killing a person who is dying.

Franciscan: A priest, brother or lay member who belongs to the religious order that follows the teachings of St. Francis of Assisi.

Genocide: Killing people because they belong to a certain racial or cultural group in an attempt to make them extinct.

Hypocritical: Describes a person who says one thing and does the opposite.

Jesuit: A priest or brother who is a member of the Society of Jesus, a religious order that does missionary and educational work.

Lay: A member of the Church who is not a priest, brother or sister.

Magnificat: Mary's song of thanksgiving to God, found in the first chapter of Luke's Gospel.

Oppression: Deliberately taking power away from a group of people.

Poverty trap: The cycle of poverty in which the poor cannot afford health care or education. Because of this, they are unable to earn enough money to help their children escape poverty.

Prophet: A person who reminds people of God's laws and God's desire for justice for all.

Racial discrimination: Treating a person badly simply because they belong to a particular race.

Social justice: Seeking fair treatment for all people and for creation.

Spiritual: Describing how God's Spirit works in people.

Stereotype: Ideas about a group based on limited or incorrect information.

Synagogue: A Jewish place of worship.

Theology: The study of God and God's relationship to the world.